I could die today and live again

poems by

Summer Farah

I could die today and live again

Copyright © 2023 by Summer Farah

ISBN: 979-8-9886654-0-3

All rights reserved. No portion of this book may be reproduced in any form without permission from the publisher, except as permitted by U.S. copyright law.

Cover design and layout by Tiffany Mallery.

Edited by MJ Malpiedi and Josh Savory.

www.gameoverbooks.com

∽ PRESS ANY BUTTON TO START ∽

9	GAME OVER
10	THE WAY THEY DANCE IN HYRULE SQUARE
13	A HISTORY OF TERMINA
14	IN ANOTHER LIFE LINK IS A POET
15	MOONCHILDREN'S LAMENT
16	INVOCATION OF THE FALSE DIVINE
17	ORIGIN OF KOROK
19	IN GERUDO VALLEY
20	SONG OF INVERTED TIME
21	IN ANOTHER LIFE LINK IS A POET
22	ODE TO THE SNOT-BUBBLE CHILD ON OUTSET ISLAND
23	INTERLUDE: PARALLEL PLAYING W/ U
24	ELEGY FOR LOST FRIENDS
25	THE WAY THEY DANCE IN HYRULE SQUARE REPRISE
26	100 YEARS SINCE THE LAST MARTYR FELL
35	MOON CHASERS EKPHRASTIC
36	IN ANOTHER LIFE LINK IS A POET (MY BROTHER LETS ME BE NAVI)
38	NOTES
41	ACKNOWLEDGEMENTS
42	BIOGRAPHY

"Such apprehension, such madness! Is the sea aware that her heroic beauty may be in disuse, someday? The moon never experienced the sinking of empires that she witnessed; day after day, she longs for a shimmering heat."— Etel Adnan, *Sea & Fog*

"I am disappointed, oh moon. I have died!" — Kamaro, *Majora's Mask*

GAME OVER

"A moon will rise out of my darkness" - Mahmoud Darwish

new moon blood moon moon with the ghastly face moon I took for granted moon that kisses the sea little moon that dilates pupils to madness I worship whatever claims to make me sane I worship sun & sky I kiss the dirt & run from bugs I respect the spider living in the window I ask what have I done to deserve this I ask what have I done to deserve this I ask what have I done to deserve there is blood in places I could have never imagined wrists rimmed with time back of palms tattooed with wisdom courage power dust moon there has always been that possibility of madness when we encounter our shadow selves every once in a cycle reflective pools reveal our dance I could die today & live again I could die today & live again I could die today & live again I could die today & live

THE WAY THEY DANCE IN HYRULE SQUARE

IT'S THE END OF THE WORLD…NO REALLY THIS TIME…I SWEAR IT I'VE HEARD THE FAMILIAR CHIMES OF THREE …THE TIMER IS COUNTING DOWN…IF YOU LOOK AT OUR LIVES WITH

THE RIGHT PERSPECTIVE…A BRIDGE DISINTEGRATES IN THE DISTANCE…LISTEN, NO, I KNOW WE'VE LIVED THIS BEFORE,   MID-SPIN…I SAW THE SHOPKEEPER'S SKIN TURN

GRAY…AND HAIR TRICKLE TO THE STONE STREETS …DO YOU REMEMBER HIM?…THE BOY WITH A FAIRY RUSHING THROUGH THE TOWN SQUARE…PEDDLING MASKS BACK & FORTH &

NOSING IN ABOUT OUR DAY?…SOMETIMES, IT FEELS LIKE ETERNITY HERE…CHOOSE YOUR FOCAL POINT: HYRULE SUN. MASK SHOPS. CLOCK TOWER. MEMORIZE: MUSIC LEAKING

FROM EACH CORRIDOR. THE BUBBLE OF CHATTER AS MERCHANTS' HORSES ARRIVE AT THE MOUTH OF TOWN… WE SPIN…WE SPIN…I FEAR WE'VE MADE THIS TURN BEFORE, THE MOON

AND SUN ARE PARALLEL AGAIN…I'VE SEEN THAT CHILD, I CAN IMAGINE HIM OLDER, TOO, SOMEHOW…IT'S LIKE HE'S HERE IN THE WHEN OF US…OUR BONES SHAKE WITH FATIGUE,

WITH AGE, OUR RE-DEAD ROTTED HEARTS KNOW THE TEMPO OF DANCE, TO PULSATE THROUGH THE SHRILLNESS BECOME OUR NECKS…OH, ALL MY LIFE I'VE WANTED LOVE.

THOUGHT IT MEANT FOCUS, A HAND TOUCHING ANOTHER. WITH NO ONE ELSE IN THE WORLD AS WE SPIN…I WANTED LOVE BUT I DID NOT WANT MY LIFE TO BE ONLY PIROUETTE

COMPLETED THROUGH WITNESS. A LIFE, TOO, IS TO GO WHERE THE SONGS DO NOT ALLOW…WHAT HAPPENS WHEN THE EYE IS BEYOND THE CASTLE WALL? WHERE AM I?

LOOK AT ME………………………………………………………………………………LOOK AT ME………………………………………………………………………LOOK AT ME……………………………………………………………………

DO YOU NEED ME TO REPEAT THAT?

[Yes]

[No]

A HISTORY OF TERMINA

In the mayor's office, men with money pretend the moon is not falling.
Laborers point to its growing shadow, poets ready their pens,
a violence is not solved without memory.
Lonely children do not cry wolf.

Laborers point to its growing shadow, poets ready their pens.
When the moon chooses its end, who will remember us here?
Lonely children do not cry wolf
while playing in the forest past nightfall, they ask—

when the moon chooses its end, who will remember us here?
They wrote songs to one another, named them for the girls
playing in the forest past nightfall, asking
what happens to lonely children with aching lungs.

They wrote songs to one another, named them for the girls
hidden away in their rooms, lit only by moon.
What happens to lonely children with aching lungs,
who yell at the falling light?

Hidden away in their rooms, lit only by moon,
men with money ignore the children
who yell at the falling light.
If it's something that can be stopped, then just try to stop it!

Men with money ignore the children
with bones growing over their face; children, shrouded in light;

if it's something that can be stopped, then just try to stop it

IN ANOTHER LIFE LINK IS A POET

shaped by need desire legend
my heart
scattered in pieces across time
zones   immortal as tradition
what am I   but goddess will?

across cliffsides I leap
towards   salvation
for me   for country
stalling at every song that leads lovers astray
mustn't forget where I am meant to be

each interlude a stolen secret
a quiet tremor   against what has already been told

long have my movements been dictated
by worn trails
trotted on by horses named for goddesses
by the familiar brush of blonde
as desert darkness looms at every signpost

me, who does not speak
until spoken to
femininity   a sword
calloused hands remember ancestry
as calloused hands touch steel
I yearn for the after   I feel it in sibling laughter,
in the house across the lake   the seclusion of water
it brings me peace it brings me death
I write this verse over and over

if the bard stops singing   of green
who am I when the last chord rings out?

oh in my fingertips   in my breath
long have I yearned for more than me for all of us

MOONCHILDREN'S LAMENT

"... Everyone has gone away, haven't they?" — Moon Child, Majora's Mask

I am so small in front of a clock tower…I am so small under the moon

It is dangerous to go alone / a prophecy as old as girlhood

And so it is night / and we are running

like we have something / to run from

Hear the crackle from A's hands / sparks like magic

Violence awes me / when shrouded by moonlight

Feet hit ground harder / than the evening warrants

I will always remember cold flush / weak knees practicing for the worst

There were so many nights after this night / when the world ended

We cried when the sun set early / we cried when our friends went away

We played music until calluses grew / until we knew who would not return

It is dangerous to go alone / there are nights I ask whispers to come true

Violence awes me / when achieved by moonlight

I am so small in front of a clock tower…I am so small under the moon

INVOCATION OF THE FALSE DIVINE

In The Legend of Zelda: Skyward Sword, Link travels between his home Skyloft, an island in the clouds, and what is known as "the surface." Zelda reveals that Skyloft was originally part of the surface world, but severed and lifted to the sky to protect the people from the threat of Demise, evil incarnate.

   O, You with voices as delicate as cloud
   O, You who fashion land from faith
      & fight from birds
   O, You with claims of goddess flesh
   There is more   There is more

     O, How the Stoned City forgets what lies beyond the thunderhead A Child disappears at night / the animals grow / feral with the growing / dusk / A Daughter presses her ear / to the grass closest / to the academy / hears the glow / of something / something / [Denial] / the ground shakes / loftwings do not fly / where they cannot see / [Denial] / O, Boundless sky / [Denial] / the Stoned City knows false / borders / [Denial] even when / the sun sets / the same pigs patrol the streets / blood is the same / Remember / [Denial] destiny intertwined / Demise comes for all / [Denial] / forgo delusion / before names become lost / before / the Stoned City falls

ORIGIN OF KOROK

Mother, I've wondered
about the fig tree
with the trunk three
arm-spans thick

>   In Kokiri forest,
>   there are Children
>   who live in houses
>   built in trees.

I know,
I know it took 100 steps to reach your house
It took another flight to your window,
the branch of the fig tree met you
where you slept

>   The Children play music to mossy rocks,
>   listen to the fog to find their way back home.
>   They are as human as they are earth.

I know your brother
begged your family to leave it be

>   Those Children fling rocks, too,
>   widdle slingshots and borrow seeds
>   from the branches nestled in their windows

I know there are families
who do not get the choice

>   *"…How sad for you that trees cannot move."*

☙
Do you grieve its leaves?
Have you tasted anything like it since?

☙
The world floods,
the world ends.

☙
Do you know I grieve its absence from my life?

☙
Zora grow wings, trees stay guardians.
Children become trees,
and the rest leave for the sea.

☙
Do you know, everywhere I go, I look for figs?
Do you know how desperately I wait for June?
Do you know why I carved them into my skin?

☙
Children become trees,
finally more earth than human

☙
Do you know if it's still there?

IN GERUDO VALLEY

                women stand tall
      henna shining in the sunlight
                    & find a husband

            women sell watermelon
              along city fountains
              curved sword in hand

          when myths come alive
                thunder crackles
    women control the heavens
in order to protect our sands

with coins adorning their ears
women leave home
& never return.

in the desert
women die
from beasts piloted by no one

in holy spaces
we adorn bodies in oil
with broken hearts
our trees our waters
even the lost join the lament

SONG OF INVERTED TIME

Oh, I know I learned songs of protection
        sang to the moon until it turned
but a tongue lost turns to smoke
        When the moon chooses its end, who will remember us here?

Sang to the moon until it turned
        I learned a song to erase the past
When the moon chooses its end, who will remember us here?
        Listen,

I learned a song to erase the past
        Bundled memories in tattered notebooks
Listen,
        what else would you choose?

Bundled memories in tattered notebooks,
        but we lost this language so long ago.
What else would you choose?
        If history never happened again?

We lost this language so long ago.
        Silent heroes become quiet civilians
if history never happened again.
        "...."

Silent heroes become quiet civilians,
        we are the lucky ones.
"...
        ..."

We are the lucky ones.
        "...
Do you need me to repeat that?
        ..."

IN ANOTHER LIFE LINK IS A POET

My beloved city. We are the lucky ones. We worship a woman immortalized by stone, her trek impossible now. Our realms are severed by sky. Oh, what blood have we forgotten? Even when the sun sets the same monsters patrol our streets. My beloved stone city, fed false borders. Oh cruel superiority, how much culture have you spoiled? Oh cruel delusions, how much blood have we forgotten? Demise comes for us all, no matter the proximity to light. History says the chosen one places foot and sword firm even before the clouds dissolve. My boundless sky, I know we used to be yours, too. There's evidence in our eyes; in candles lit for weddings; with the word for spiders. Please, before the stone city falls, Goddess forgive us for our hubris. Forgive us for us, with even our wells drowned in history, our names dedicated to myth, dedicated to easier passage. Please, let every realm return to how we were. Let earth rejoin sky. Return and become more. Please, my beloved city, want it, still.

ODE TO THE SNOT-BUBBLE CHILD ON OUTSET ISLAND

for noelle

There is mucus bubbling
at the base of your nose.
You scream when I clean your face.

We have to walk
before we can run.
Know your legs first,
then sprint.

And yet, you sprint,
And so, I follow.

Who can blame you?
Your body is yours, and has only been around for so long.
Who is to say
this is not just part of growing up?
There is so much that
they will try to take from you.
Today, we let boogers be the worst.

Dear one. Your face is meant to be clean.
Your water is meant to be clear.
Your future is meant to be yours.

I am prepared to brave the forest
for you.
Wait for me.

INTERLUDE: PARALLEL PLAYING W/ U

for jess

forgive me. i am forgetting that which is good / in service / of narrative. / in the needle aisle of a craft store i confess *i am afraid of getting close to someone again.* lines crease the corner of my eyes / phantom laughter / relics of the voices i will not hear again, unless / the worlds are small. / each made up of archetypes / repeated across titles&endcards / but not within / in this lifetime there is a princess & a hero / no more / no less / in the next there will be too, / unless / consider: the end of the map / where the rock walls blur / & the abyss endless / costing ¼ heart with each fall. / again, again, i try / i want to know what lies at the bottom / consider, the abyss: a reset point. / selves that always return / to the ledge how lonely it can be / to be a certain type of character. singular purpose. looped dialogue. how lucky am i to find someone / who slots into the same role / a friendship can be found / in serendipity / of reading the same story at the same time / without the other knowing / found in sitting side-by-side / i play on the tv & you play handheld & the humm of our systems are complementary / the gentlest of silences / habit / found in i watch a show & you will exist next to me / until, we wait for the next season, together /& the gentlest of silences filled by shared guilt / we talk of the unmeasurable weight / of wanting to do good / twinned in our overwhelm / of how to serve / well / of how to be kind, & disbelief / in those who won't do the same / we can practice here / & consider, the space between two couch cushions: the smallest of worlds / teach me your obsessions for when i miss you most / & i will help you fight monsters in the depths / pray i look cool / even if i fuck up / tell me tell me tell me / about your progress / in that other game / & i promise i won't ruin the rest / consider: the sequel grants us who gravitate towards the edge / second chance / a curious reward / another kingdom / to touch / instead of / please tell me & tell me & tell me / we'll never get tired of this

ELEGY FOR LOST FRIENDS

In The Legend of Zelda: Link Between Worlds, Link travels between his familiar Hyrule and its parallel Lorule, a land that has descended into darkness.

oh

my friend

my friend, i fou-

ght to make my life

yours heart steeped in li-

ght my back flush to walls sudd-

ddenly, suddenly all of the worst worlds

come true i worship ancient roots i thought

i s-   ch-

aw tendrils   aos in us

grow from yo-   still my friend

ur skin just as mine how   i will miss you as you

many of us can say we are free   are gone even when you exist

from cruelty? of course we hold   in the back of my mind ravaged by

no tenderness each time i step outside   cruelty i shattered so much stored light

something dies at my feet oh understand the in each piece if only you had it too

THE WAY THEY DANCE IN HYRULE SQUARE
REPRISE

THERE IS A HOUSE BY THE RIVERBANK
YOU FILL WITH RELICS THAT STAY GIFTS
SWORDS THAT NEVER NEED REPAIR
COLORS THAT DO NOT REMIND YOU OF WAR

YOU REACH OUT TENTATIVELY
THIS CYCLICAL DANCE
TURN WITH NO MIND TO DESTINY
ACCORDIONS BLARE
AS THEY HAVE FOR CENTURIES

A LIGHT PIERCES
THROUGH THE SKY

THE AIR IS SWEET
YOU HAVE NOTHING TO FEAR

NIGHT IS HERE

THERE IS NOTHING TO FEAR

100 YEARS SINCE THE LAST MARTYR FELL

Legend of Zelda: Breath of the Wild begins with a memory-less Link awakening from a 100-year-slumber induced by Zelda. This is a last resort, to ensure there is hope left, after all of the other Champions chosen to fight the looming evil of Ganon's Calamity are killed by his various forms. Link ultimately faces Ganon with the spirit of each Champion at his side.

                                R E J O I C E , P E O P L E

                                      SOLDIERS SING

T H E C A L A M I T Y H A S B E E N C O N T A I N E D

AS IF WE ARE TO PAY NO HEED TO THE SWARMS AT NIGHT

THE SHADOW IN THE CORNER OF YOUR EYE

NAMELESS TRAVELERS ROAMING THE STREETS IN PLACE OF OUR OWN

THE COST OF WOOD HAS GONE DOWN

OUR TREES GROW WITH THE BLOOD MOON

ROOTS OVERTAKING GODDESS KNOWS WHAT

WE CAN ONLY TAKE SO MUCH LOSS

SOMETIMES WE FORGET OUR OWN THRESHOLD

SOMETIMES GRIEF IS A RESET TINGED IN RED

SOMETIMES ALL OF OUR RESISTANCE IS

UNDONE WHEN NIGHTFALL COMES

BUT WE WILL NEVER FORGET

CHAMPIONS LEAVE MEMORIES IN SUNLIGHT

IF YOU CLOSE YOUR EYES IN THE SHIMMER

YOU CAN FEEL THEIR BREATH ON YOUR SKIN

TASTE FIGS RETAKEN IN AFTERLIFE

SWEETNESS MOST DESERVED

ESPECIALLY AFTER THE LONGEST OF SLUMBERS

WE REMEMBER THEIR NAMES

T

HEALERS SHOT IN ACTION WE REMEMBER THEIR NAMES CHILDREN THROW ROCKS AT MECHANICAL BEASTS WE REMEMBER THEIR NAMES AN UNCLE DISAPPEARED BY THE BORDER WE REMEMBER THEIR NAMES TEMPLES LOST REMEMBER THEIR NAMES OLIVE TREES UPROOTED REMEMBER THEIR NAMES EVEN WHEN MALICE CRUSTS THE ENTRANCE TO OUR MOST HOLY PLACES WE REMEMBER THEIR NAMES STILL REMEMBER THEIR NAMES O EACH DAY WE EXCHANGE HEART FOR GODDESS WILL PRAY FOR DEMISE TO END WAIT FOR MOTHERS TO RETURN WRITE SONGS OF WIND & CHAMPIONS WHO RODE IT WE REMEMBER THEIR NAMES LET THEM GIVE US STRENGTH CALL TO OUR CHAMPIONS IN TIMES MOST DEPLETED WE RESIST LURES OF CAPITAL & FALSE SAFETY REFUSE BORDERS THAT DIVIDE OUR RIVERS REFUSE ANY LANGUAGE THAT REMAPS OUR HISTORIES WE MUST REMEMBER THEIR NAMES REMEMBER

THEIR NAMES REMEMBER THEIR NAMES REMEMBER
THEIR NAMES REMEMBER THEIR NAMES REMEMBER
THEIR NAMES REMEMBER THEIR NAMES REMEMBER
EIR NAMES THEIR REMEMBER THEIR NAMES REMEMBER
THEIR NAMES REMEMBER THEIR NAMES REMEMBER
THEIR NAMES REMEMBER THEIR NAMES REMEMBER
THEIR NAMES REMEMBER THEIR NAMES REMEMBER
THEIR NAMES REMEMBER THEIR NAMES REMEMBER
EIR NAMES REMEMBER THEIR NAMES REMEMBER
THEIR NAMES REMEMBER THEIR NAMES REMEMBER
THEIR NAMES REMEMBER THEIR NAMES REMEMBER
THEIR NAMES REMEMBER THEIR NAMES REMEMBER
THEIR NAMES REMEMBER THEIR NAMES REMEMBER
THEIR NAMES REMEMBER THEIR NAMES REMEMBER

NAMES, O–

DO YOU NEED ME TO REPEAT THAT?
    [Yes]
    [No]

MOON CHASERS EKPHRASTIC

A clouded night. But still, your light persists. A girl runs and runs until her legs no longer suffice. A family shuffles into the car, eyes towards you. Up, they drive. The air here is so unfamiliar that they have almost forgotten wind. Its call, in tandem with moon, revives. It has been so long since we felt alive. Tonight, you are brighter; tonight, you are closer, closer, closer. You have an ancient name, one recalled only on extraordinary evenings, a name that reminds us we too are guilty of theft. Up, up, towards the cloudless peak. People crowd the streets to try to capture your form, beg for a closeness that cannot come. This distance aches, and yet. It is the middle of summer. There are no deer left to lend their names. Absences, absences; wolves howl in their place, domesticated kin join too. Wildness, they have forgotten. Will a symphony calm your light? Will a symphony stop us from trying? If only, if only; to catch up with the moon is to let it take your breath. To catch up with the moon is to start all over again.

IN ANOTHER LIFE LINK IS A POET
(MY BROTHER LETS ME BE NAVI)

i have only been afraid of the moon once   grew obsessed with its glare before i could read painted flowers around its face each year / until even my anxiety turned beautiful.   have you ever wondered if you were loved or just needed?   before girlhood taught necessity   b e f o r e girlhood taught service we are children, in a basement in michigan. my brother lets me be navi / n64 controller connected / to nothing   i am child in its best form, / blissed / i am helping. in reality, / company. let's hear it for the lonely children for without there would be no game a boy without a fairy, until he is not / LINK, until he is me / girl, until i am not / a lifetime of favors turns into a lifetime / of favors.   when there is no one left to give to / what will i be? / all my life i've loved hills / i sit at their crests & beg my mother / for us to go home / in front of the only house i'd yet known / she says *not having a country is like   not having a mother*   / consider   the children of the forest / motherless / the boy without a fairy / until / children without a country / until   t h e midwest is so, so green /   california can be, too / i forget / palestine /   there are hills i've loved all my life   made myself sick rolling down them   asking grass to stain me green / oh heroes / i had so many before i could speak of why / saria sounds like samar &   / i want to be loved by trees / canonized by wind   learn songs that slow all of us down / i long for a history / as concrete as the story that plays / before i press start / i walk up a mountain after i spend hours climbing mountains &   i mean, i walk uphill after i spend hours playing / i have been weak / bed-ridden / a refrain   *i just feel so crazy all of the time* / i am the smallest / i have ever been / monotony, monotony, a song i am afraid of learning / past nightfall / i play until i hear the stable song or / past moonlight / until i hand my brother the controller or / until everyone is watching us / fight / together / slowly   until my battery dies / until i am child   again

NOTES

GAME OVER
The epigraph comes from Mahmoud Darwish's poem "Inanna's Milk"; the version I reference is translated by Munir Akash and Carolyn Forche.

THE WAY THEY DANCE IN HYRULE SQUARE
This poem is with thanks to Farrokhzad & Hozier & the Lovers in *Ocarina of Time* and *Majora's Mask*. I was always so afraid of the zombies/redeads that appear in Hyrule Square during the adult phase of *OoT* that I forgot to be envious of all of the joy in the child phase, until I grew up and N64 graphics were no longer impressive enough to make me afraid, but they were still perfect enough to depict love. I want only be made perfectly in tune with another. Players will recall the wordy Owl that asks, "Did you get all that?" If you rush, you'll instinctually hit A, and it will all repeat again. I learned to slow down and take it all in, just once. Or, you can reread the poems as many times as you need.

A HISTORY OF TERMINA
In *Majora's Mask*, the moon is falling. If you go into the mayor's office on Day 1, there is a conversation between him and the construction boss; they don't think the town needs to be evacuated, despite the fact the moon has the scariest fucking face you could imagine and is clearly too close for comfort. Each day that passes, the town rumbles and rumbles closer to midnight. So much of this game is about loss, including the mechanics; to save everyone, you have to reset. They have to forget what you've done. To save your progress, they have to forget, and you go back to Day 1. Did any of it even happen? Who is sacrificed into silence in order for denial to continue? The powerful are discomforted by the lonely at best, want them disappeared at worst. I wrote so much of this book while sick, much of it feeling lonely. But the moon only stays in the sky when the four giants come together—unity. As Skull Kid says, *if it's something that can be stopped, then just try to stop it.*

IN ANOTHER LIFE LINK IS A POET
In *Breath of the Wild*, I am struck by the silences, the white space, the emptiness the player can choose whether or not they wish to fill. You can go straight to Ganon, 3 hearts, speed-runners' wet dream.

Or, you can delay for hundreds of hours, the only concern is Zelda holding off Ganon alone nagging at the back of your mind—but only if you let yourself get so invested. But, if you don't allow yourself that, what else is there?

MOON CHILDREN'S LAMENT
Whenever I felt a certain type of homesick/academically overwhelmed/general malaise/hysteria my freshman year of college, I would walk campus at night. I liked the cold bay area wind and the dark shadows Berkeley trees cast on the pavement. I would stand under the clocktower and feel small enough for whatever violent whirring that was happening in my brain to calm down. Endless love to *Majora's Mask*'s moon children, the little freaks.

ORIGIN OF KOROK
Perhaps it is nostalgia fueled, but *Ocarina of Time* and *Wind Waker* feel like canonical Zelda games, to me. I don't mean canonical in the sense that they happened, or anything to do with the timeline—rather, culturally. I am endlessly fascinated by the evolution of the Kokiri to the Korok, of Zora to Rito. I think of metaphors in which Indigenous Palestinians are the land, we are the olive tree—what are the children of the forest if not the extreme of this motif? "…How sad for you that trees cannot move." is a direct quote from the Deku tree himself.

IN GERUDO VALLEY
The Gerudo are a race of desert-dwelling, Amazonian-esque women that appear in many Zelda titles. From early racist depictions as a villainous people that produces the Truest Evil of them all, Ganondorf, to a seemingly reparative, vibrant, fully-fleshed out society in *Tears of the Kingdom*, I am always conflicted when I head to fulfill whatever quest I have to in their corner of the map. And yet, this is the poem I came to.

SONG OF INVERTED TIME
Majora's Mask is a timed game; one way to make it less stressful is to play the Song of Inverted Time, which "slows the flow of time" and gives you more time to fulfill quests and temples. It's vital! But it doesn't show up in the Menu screen where all of your other learned songs to; I always have to ask my brother to remind me how to play it.

IN ANOTHER LIFE LINK IS A POET
This *Skyward Sword*-inspired poem is an ode, plea, love letter to my beloved city. May Nazareth and all of 48 be reunited with our kin. From the river to the sea.

ODE TO THE SNOT-BUBBLE CHILD ON OUTSET ISLAND
I love this NPC in *Wind Waker*, who also appears in *Minish Cap*. Babies are so silly when you try to clean their nose during their first cold, as if the addition of snot is the same as growing a new tooth. I love you, Nounou.

INTERLUDE: PARALLEL PLAYING W/ U
"Parallel play" refers to when toddlers/children play by themselves side-by-side. I do this as a woman in her mid 20s. "Another kingdom to touch" takes inspiration from Aracelis Girmay's line in "Kingdom Animalia," "I am telling you / a true thing. This is the only kingdom. / The kingdom of touching;" and "tell me tell me tell me" takes inspiration from Wendy Xu's "WE ARE BOTH SURE TO DIE," "Please tell me and tell me and tell / me about the river." The games referenced are *Breath of the Wild* and *Tears of the Kingdom*.

ELEGY FOR LOST FRIENDS
Link Between Worlds is one of the most underrated Zelda games. I am always thinking about the what-ifs, if everything was the same but one thing, if something had just been a little different, where would I be, where would we be, would X be here still, and on and on.

100 YEARS SINCE THE LAST MARTYR FELL
Palestinians call each of our own murdered by the Zionist regime "martyr". The blood moon mechanism, while useful for farming monster parts for monster upgrades, is devastating in practice, and what it means for resistance. *Tears of the Kingdom* explores this futility gracefully.

MOONCHASERS' EKPHRASTIC
Ekphrasis of a video I took one night that my parents & I drove to see the moon.

ACKNOWLEDGEMENTS

Gratitude to the editors & journals that previously published versions of these poems—

GAME OVER (as PORTRAIT OF EACH MOON THAT HAS SEEN LINK LIVE) in *Poetry Online*
IN GERUDO VALLEY & MOON CHILDREN'S LAMENT in *Long Con Magazine*
IN ANOTHER LIFE LINK IS A POET in *[lock-on]*
INTERLUDE: PARALLEL PLAYING W/ U, IN ANOTHER LIFE LINK IS A POET, MOON CHASERS' EKPHRASTIC & A HISTORY OF TERMINA in *Guernica*

Thank you to MJ & Josh & the *Game Over Books* squad; without your excitement & support, this would have been a rushed little zine that died on my ko-fi page. Thank you to my Tin House group: Samia, Mónica, Urvashi, Sally, Sara, Mariam, Nicole, and the most wonderful instructor anyone could have wished for, Leila; without you, I could not have imagined this project to be interesting to anyone but myself.

Thank you to the loved ones who reacted kindly and enthusiastically each time I posted a little draft, thank you to the loved ones who read the abundance of versions of my "ZELDA POEMS RUNNING DRAFT" Google doc, thank you to the loved ones who made me more excited about making this real: Nico, Marlin, George, Leena, Sarah, Fargo, Helen, Jess, Lee, Blue, Tegan, Gabe, Cassie, Jillian, Kendall, Pan, Nathanial, Melanie, Madi, Cameron, Sarah, Kiki, Noor, Christine, Rasha, Samah, Nadia, Laurel, Tarik, Kiana, Umang, Ame, Alyssa, and all my RAWI family. Thank you to my cover artist, Tiffany, for the weird little guys on the moon. Thank you Jess Rizkallah, my poetsister. Thank you to my actual brother, Hani, for playing games with me, and our parents for enabling us.

I owe so much to the art that I spent time with in the years of working on this little book: thank you Shigeru Miyamoto, thank you Mitski, thank you Hozier, thank you Koji Kondo, thank you Lip Manegio, thank you Sennah Yee, thank you Etel Adnan, thank you Rina Sawayama, thank you Hanif Abdurraqib, thank you Richard Siken, thank you Melissa Lozada-Oliva, thank you Lorde, thank you Lord Huron, thank you Mary Oliver, thank you David Lowry's *The Green Knight*, and thank you to my very real friends Link and Zelda.

BIOGRAPHY

Summer Farah is a Palestinian American writer based in California. She organizes with the Radius of Arab American Writers and is a member of the National Book Critics Circle. She edited the folio *ORIGINALITYISDEAD* for *Violet, Indigo, Blue, Etc.*, served as the poetry editor for the *FIYAH* Palestine Solidarity issue, and wrote the monthly column *POETRY DOUBLE FEATURES* for Palette Poetry. A fan of the CW series *Supernatural*, she is in the top .01% of Mitski listeners on Spotify.